# MY MOTHER'S KEEPER

A Daughter's Struggle with

Balancing Love, Care, and Protection

for her Mother Battling Dementia

By

**Kimberly J. Richardson**

# *Contents*

# *Dedication*

*This book is dedicated to my beloved mother, Laura Jean Wright.*

*Mom, thank you for showing me at an early age, your strength, your love, your beauty, and your servant's heart. I watched you care for me and my brothers and sister with such grace and ease that only a mother could give. I saw how you studied and worked hard which helped develop in me my thirst for learning and strong work ethic. I paid attention when you dressed us for church on Sunday mornings. You taught me to act like a lady with my fancy hat, button-jacket top, pleated skirt, white gloves, and patent-leather shoes. I was a witness to your service in ministry, your assistance with elders in the neighborhood, and your political activism. You fought a long and tough battle in the end, but you carried the badge of honor from the very beginning.*

*Love your daughter,*
*Kimberly*

*This book is also dedicated to every family that is currently dealing with or have lost a loved one to Dementia and Alzheimer's Disease.*

*And, to all the healthcare professionals, hospice network, homecare aides, caregivers, volunteers, social workers and others who are committed to the care and welfare of others.*

*In gratitude,*
*Kimberly*

*Be kindly affectionate to one another with brotherly love, in honor giving preference to one another; not lagging in diligence, fervent in spirit, serving the Lord; rejoicing in hope, patient in tribulation, continuing steadfastly in prayer; distributing to the needs of the saints, given to hospitality.*

~ Romans 12:10-13 ~

# *Acknowledgements*

Giving honor and glory to my Lord and Savior Jesus Christ for keeping me, guiding me, and giving me the patience and fortitude to write this book.

A heartfelt thank you to my husband, my friend, my rock, Donald Richardson, for being supportive from the start and during the countless hours I spent working through the days and nights. Thank you for allowing me space to create.

To my sons, DonLarae and Dijon Richardson, thank you for being a reflection of the values instilled in you; Respectful; Self-Motivated, Hardworking; Family-Oriented; Educated; Loving; Conscious; Service-Minded; and Godly black men. Thank you for encouraging me and bringing me so much Joy!

Giving honor to my Pastor Sam Moore and Lady LaShawn Moore of Conqueror's Church for helping me grow spiritually, and to my Conqueror's Church family for your selfless commitment to service.

To Charlotte Howard, Founder and CEO of Heart Centered Women Publishing for creating a platform for women to share their story through writing, and speaking. Thank you for your unwavering commitment in helping me fulfill my dream of not only writing my solo book, but building my business around helping others share their stories by writing their books.

To Pam Perry for seeing my drive and potential and selecting me to be a participant in your Branding Accelerator Cohort program. You were the teacher that appeared at the time I was ready. Thank you for your mentoring and your commitment to helping so many women and men have a voice.

To Dr. Venus Opal Reese and your team of Accelerators, Terry Houze, Angie Watkins, Teresa Crawford, and Rochele Lawson for helping me see the value in my message, for lessons on accountability, personal integrity, and for helping me create the emotional atmosphere for healing and manifestation and, thank you to all of my BWM sisters for uplifting and keeping each other encouraged throughout our entrepreneurial journey.

Thank you to Kimberly Ramsawak of Professional Jetsetters Academy for planting the seed that sparked my entrepreneurial quest.

To my brother, Donald Williams, for keeping our family lifted in prayer during our mother's illness. To my sister, Nichole Wright, for your business acumen, and constant support and words of encouragement throughout this journey. To my sister in law, Sharon Williams, for all the times you did Laura's hair and the love shown with assisting in her care. To my brother, Jeffery Williams, thank you for the many uplifting calls of praise and gratitude. To my brother, Carlton Wright, for persevering and not giving up.

To my father, Carl Wright, for raising me as your daughter. Thank you for the love you gave to our family, in spite of the difficult times. To my in-laws, Curtis and Martha Richardson, thank you for your endearing love and support. To my Uncle Jerry and Aunt Verna, thank you for always opening your arms and loving us unconditionally.

To my dear friend, whom I love like a sister, Wanda Lee-Stevens. Thank you for a lifetime of friendship. To the close and personal friends of the family, who are like brothers and sisters to me, you know who you are. I love you all. To all my uncles and aunties and cousins, and nieces, and nephews that are too many to mention, know that I love you all and am grateful for the impact you've made in my life as well as Laura's.

A special thank you to Ms. Connie Waters for the many years of love and support you've given Laura. Thank you for being a friend to the end. Thank you to Louise Verbeke, Barbara, Carolyn and Wayne Peoples, Linda, and Mildred. Thank you to cousin Brenda Pullins for helping me drive Laura to Oklahoma for our family reunion. We had a great ride and great time and, to cousin Kathy Morgan for opening your home and giving up your master suite for me and Laura. I love you dearly.

Finally, to my grandchildren, Jayden, Jordyn, Paetyon, Devon, and soon to arrive, Sire, I hope this book inspires you to continue the legacy bestowed upon you. May you hold dear and cherish this book for all your days.

Love NaNa Kim.

# *"Better Safe than Sorry"*
## *Chapter One*

It was November 2008. We had just moved mom to an Assisted Living Facility. Her safety and well-being had been in jeopardy. Mom had another episode. This time, she was found leaning outside her fifth-floor balcony screaming for help! According to reports from management, mom was inside her apartment eating. After choking on some food, she became alarmed and believed someone was trying to poison her. Passer-bye's alerted management who then notified me after calling for emergency assistance. It was only a few weeks before that mom had passed out in the lobby after exiting the apartment elevator. Again, emergency was called and she was taken to the hospital just minutes away. Tests showed that her blood pressure was extremely high. This wasn't something new. Hypertension was something that mom was able to manage with blood pressure medication for many, many years. Nevertheless, the recent diagnosis of Dementia about a year ago, didn't help matters. With minimum supervision, mom was still able to live on her own. She was able to bathe, dress herself, walk to the nearby shops, and prepare some of her meals.

Laura had the most beautiful legs that complimented her five-foot seven physique. Her smile could light up a room. Never lacking attention from men, she caught the attention of a male admirer named Adrian who lived in the unit next door. Adrian adored mom.

Mom liked him also. We trusted him with her. They began a courtship over time. They loved to hang out at her place and listen to his collection of jazz CDs. The fact that he was able to drive and get around provided an outlet for mom, especially when we were not around. One day, she had him drive her around to see her kids. He drove to the eastside of Detroit so she could visit with me and family.

I was pleasantly surprised. Adrian mentioned that they stopped by the liquor store on the west side looking for my brother, Jeffery who worked there at one time. She was managing her meds during this time. The dementia medication seemed to have slowed the progression of her confusion and cognitive decline. Mom still had her wits about her. She still had clarity about things. We had a system in place that worked well for a little over a year. I would call her every morning so she could take her morning meds, and again in the evening. Her meds were strategically placed in a weekly pill container labeled Sunday thru Saturday.

There was a color-coded pink for morning and color-coded blue for evening. A couple of days per week, she went to the Friends Adult Day Care that I got her enrolled into. She didn't seem all that excited about going, but she did stick with it for a few months. I would call to make sure she was up and dressed. The daycare provided transportation to pick her up and take her to and from the facility on her designated days.

Mom was able to leave on her own and lock the door. With purse in hand, she would walk to the elevator which was a few steps away and ride down to the lobby. When exiting and entering her apartment building, she would mingle with the other residents sitting nearby. This really made a difference in her stability. Having a social life is so key to a person's well-being. It took some of the pressure off me and my brother and sister. Especially since we all worked very demanding jobs and still had children at home to raise.

# *"A Family Affair"*

## *Chapter Two*

Laura, wasn't always like this. She was a vivacious, intelligent, active, hard-working mother and wife who raised five children. She actually had six children, three boys and three girls. By birth is Donald, nicknamed 'Punchy', me, Jeffery, then Alissa (Lisa), Carlton and Nichole (Nikki). Our sister, Lisa, died from pneumonia when she was about ten months old. Momma kept a clipping of Lisa's hair in a bible when we were kids. I remember, at least a couple of times, of opening the bible to the exact page of Lisa's hair and touching her soft, black, curly braid.

Mom was married nearly 25 years to my stepfather, Carl. I remember when they got married in my grandmother's living room in Tulsa, Oklahoma. I was about three or four at the time. It wasn't long before mom, Punchy, me, Jeffery and Carlton were aboard a train heading to the Motor City to reunite with Carl, our dad. My sister, Nikki, wasn't born until several years later. Dad, who was a cook in the army, just finished serving in Vietnam. He went to Detroit ahead of us to secure a job with the Ford Motor Company, an automobile manufacturing plant. I still have some memory of the train ride, like eating oatmeal for breakfast. To this day, I feel a warm, soothing comfort every time I hear a train sound its horn in the distance.

Growing up, family life had more good times than bad. We traveled together by car to visit momma's family who were spread between Oklahoma, Kansas and Texas and my father's family who lived in Arkansas and Ohio. Mom was the second oldest of five girls and two brothers. By birth, was Aunt Sissy, momma, Aunt Etta, Aunt Bell, Uncle Mike, Aunt Wanda, and Uncle Junior. Our traveling was usually to Tulsa, Oklahoma to see my grandmother whom we affectionately called 'Ma Dear'. She died from lung cancer when I was 24 years old. Aunt Sissy died about 16 years later after having weight loss surgery.

I remember momma telling me that she had just spoken with Aunt Sissy before the scheduled procedure, and told her not to do it. I thought it was because Aunt Sissy always had some kind of health issue. I would learn much later that her doctor warned against it. She went through with the procedure anyway. She died weeks later from infection. Mom was really sad. She and Sissy had a close relationship. They talked on the phone a lot. Mom kept in contact with all her siblings, even though they didn't see each other for years at a time. She always enjoyed traveling and getting together for family reunions.

Having a natural talent for home décor, mom loved decorating our home. She hung wallpaper with precision, matching the seams so effortlessly that you couldn't tell when one sheet ended and another began.

Our dining room was decorated in a burnt orange velvety textured wallpaper that matched the burnt orange carpet.

Our dining room table was black with a textured top, shaped like an octagon with six matching orange leather swivel chairs with a black rod-iron base. The upstairs full bath was decorated in red with matching shower curtain and bath rugs. It really complimented the black and white ceramic tile that outlined the walls surrounding the tub and sink. I'll never forget the clock that hung on the wall above the mirrored medicine cabinet. It was the shape of a black cat whose eyes would move from side to side with each tick of the clock.

We always enjoyed playing family board games like monopoly, checkers, and scrabble. We also had plenty of books to read. Mom always had a subscription of Reader's Digest, Ebony and Jet Magazines. I remember a handful collection of books by Donald Goines, a popular local black author. There was this one book I loved reading, titled "Black Girl Lost". It was an urban tale about a girl named Sandra who had to fend for herself on the streets of Detroit. It was easy to relate to because I was a black girl living in Detroit and surviving. We also had a collection of Britannica Encyclopedias at our disposal that came in handy when doing homework and book reports. It was our modern-day version of what 'Google' is in the 21$^{st}$ Century.

But, like most families, we had our share of dysfunction. Most of it stemmed from my father's weekend bouts of drinking, gambling and smoking weed. Dad worked his weekly afternoon shifts Monday thru Friday faithfully at the plant. He loved to drink and party most weekends.

There were times that dad would leave to go play cards, then return home after drinking expecting to get more money. I guess mom would hide her money or money that was set aside to pay bills. When she refused to give it to dad or tell him where it was, he would assault her physically. Sometimes the assault just happened in a fit of anger, but it was always after he'd been drinking. Mom packed all five of us kids in the car on a couple of occasions, in an attempt to leave him. She'd drive all the way to Tulsa to Ma dear's house, in the dead of winter. After about a week, she'd drive us all back home to Detroit. I left home at the age of nineteen with my three-month-old son, DonLarae.

I was told to leave by momma. Though--at the same time--I couldn't wait to get out on my own! Life at home became unbearable. I became the center of focus of everything that was wrong at home. I was working at Popeye's Chicken when I found out I was pregnant. A few months later, I was laid-off after informing management of my "condition". I applied for unemployment benefits, and was later denied after management lied and said I was fired. I didn't fight it. I was able to get some financial assistance from Social Services to help me pay rent to mom and dad. I also received food assistance for me and the baby. One day, I felt the need to speak my mind, in a letter to momma. She wasn't having it! We didn't even have a conversation. She just sternly told me to be gone by the time she got home from work.

I honestly believe now that mom knew I was capable of making it on my own.

She knew that I would be a good mother to my child. I once overheard her tell my Aunt Verna one day that I did a good job with caring for my child. Mom knew that my boyfriend and father of my child—Donald, had my back. He had been my saving grace, when they seemed to be oblivious to my emotional despair. My relationship with my mother was more or less a friendship than it was a mother-daughter bond.

Mom wasn't the hugs and kisses type. Nor did she verbally express her love, but I knew she loved me in her own special way. Like, during the times she would press my hair after washing and braiding it the day before when I was about eleven years old. She would give me "the talk" about menstruation and boys. Or, when she would order my favorite Dr. Seuss books that came in the mail. Still, for many years, I felt like the "black sheep" of the family. So, I buried my emotions by staying active in school, reading books, studying, and hanging out with my friends.

I was in my thirties before I realized, looking back, that mom was in survival mode. In a deeper sense, her telling me to leave, was actually her way of protecting me from all the chaos. She couldn't fight for me, and her, and her husband, and the other remaining children. To God Be the Glory! Several years would pass before Carl and Laura separated, eventually divorcing.

# "A Will and A Way"

## Chapter Three

Mom worked in the skilled trades industry. In 2005, she was laid-off from her contract job with American Axle. She had owned her home for about five years or so. With the help of my brother, Carlton, mom was able to make some upgrades to the home's exterior. She added a two-car garage and had a porch built off the rear of the house. Mom loved working in the yard and tending to her flowers. In 2006, her unemployment benefits ran out. She applied for work elsewhere and did a brief stint with a couple of jobs, but wasn't able to sustain them for long. The drive became too much with one, and the other required long periods of standing without rest. I remember the conversation we had on the phone about that. It was an office cleaning job. She expressed that she was only allowed a half hour lunch break for a six or seven-hour shift and that being on her feet for long periods was becoming too much. I told her that it was too long for her to be on her feet and that she didn't need to work under those conditions.

Her only source of income now came from her small pension with General Dynamics, a job she worked for fifteen years, nearly thirty years earlier. By the time we found out about her situation, foreclosure proceedings were already underway.

My sister visited her one day and saw that mom barely had food in the refrigerator.

Nikki began to go through mom's bills and finances to look for ways to assist. She also bought her groceries on several occasions. I spoke with the mortgage company in hopes of remedying the current situation.

There was an option to do what is called a "Deed in lieu of foreclosure" in which mom would have to voluntarily transfer the title of the property to the bank in exchange for a release from the mortgage obligation. We had to first make an attempt to sell the property. So, I contacted a realtor to put the house on the market in hopes that it would sell for more than what was owed on the property.

Mom had already pulled the equity out of the property unbeknownst to us. We voiced our opinion regarding her home purchase from the beginning. We believed the home was overpriced to not have had a back porch, a paved driveway or a garage. The home did have its plus side, however. The basement was a nice size. She had a walk-in storage closet, a large utility room that housed the washer and dryer with plenty of open space. There was a separate living area that mom set up like a living room and bedroom.

She always made it nice and cozy. I just loved her talent for decorating. I'm sure I inherited my love and talent for home decor from her. I had an opportunity to retile her kitchen floor by giving it an earthy wooden floor look to match the cabinetry. Mom was happy. She loved the neighborhood and its location.

During this time, something else was happening. The housing market was changing. Home buyers were no longer interested in purchasing older homes when they could pay a little extra for a newly built one. The market for newer homes was steadily on the rise. This made it even more difficult to sell her home.

By now, mom's sleeping habits had changed as she grew increasingly agitated and stressed. She would be found curled up on her loveseat in the den, day and night. Albeit, it was her TV room, but it was the all night that was disturbing. She pretty much stopped sleeping in her bed. We became increasingly concerned about her health and well-being. One day, I went to check on mom.

As I approached the back door to unlock it, I found the door already open and unlocked. I assumed mom was gone because her car was not in the driveway. Somewhat alarmed, I searched the house to find that it was indeed empty. Mom had left the door open and unlocked. I waited for her return to make sure everything was okay. When I talked to her about it later, mom expressed that she believed something was wrong with her. She made reference to her memory and how she went to a doctor recently in hopes of being approved for Social Security Disability. She said the doctor told her there was nothing wrong with her.

We began to prepare mom for a new reality. We wanted her to never have to worry about working to keep a roof over her head.

Senior housing communities were sprawling up all over the Metro Detroit area. In a few months, she would be eligible to draw her social security. It appeared to be a win-win!

# *"From Bad to Worse"*

## *Chapter Four*

By November, 2006, we packed mom's belongings and moved her into a Senior Apartment in Lansing, Michigan. Approximately 70 miles outside Detroit, this was further out than I had planned, but agreed to because this is where Nikki and my nephew Justin resided. After looking at several senior apartments near the area mom loved in Detroit, she turned them all down. She just wasn't interested. According to Nikki, the senior apartments in Lansing were newer, and less costly when compared to the Detroit area. Thinking that a change of scenery would be good for mom, it was a go, especially since she was willing.

We got her situated. Nikki would check in on her daily after getting off from work. The area was nicely landscaped and not far from downtown Lansing. Mom's apartment was small but nice. It had new carpet, a balcony with a view of the open landscape, a large full bath, and a nice sized bedroom. It wasn't long before mom began to exhibit signs of deep depression. She went from bad to worse! She stopped calling her friends. She stopped eating her meals on a regular. Mom began to shut down! When we moved her, she was still able to drive.

The change proved to be too much for her! I didn't realize how big the impact of losing her home would be. Mom felt ashamed! She was angry with us for not doing more to save her home.

Nikki made an appointment for mom to be examined by a psychiatrist. She enlisted the assistance of our older brother, Punchy to come to Lansing and escort mom to the doctor for a psych evaluation. The doctor diagnosed mom with severe depression and psychosis. He prescribed the anti-psychotic Abilify and Remeron medication. He stressed the importance of eating throughout the day. Upon a follow-up visit, mom had not made much improvement. The doctor threatened to have her admitted if she didn't put forth the effort to get better. He explained the medicine would not work if she didn't eat.

He recommended that she go outside for about 15 minutes a day and just walk around the apartment complex to get some fresh air and exercise. Mom also had a major vitamin deficiency due to her poor diet. To make matters worse, she began to hallucinate. She believed that a lady was hitting her with a stick while she slept at night. One day, I spent the night at her place. I wanted to see what she did at night. Would she sleep all through the night? Was she a threat to herself? Why did she have these brown spots on her beautiful light brown skin? The evening came. I helped her get ready for bed. She was hesitant about going to sleep. I assured her that everything would be alright. That I would be right there if she needed me. Mom had a one-bedroom apartment. So, I slept on the couch that night.

I thought about sleeping with her in her bed so she would feel safe, but I wanted to see what really happens at night while she slept. I wanted to make sure no one was entering her apartment at night. I waited for her to fall off to sleep before I eventually nodded off.

I don't remember how much time had passed before I awoke and found mom standing over me in the middle of the night. Startled, I stared up at her not sure what she was doing. I asked her if she was okay. I believed she nodded. I got up and walked her back to her room. I turned on the light so she could see that there was nothing or no one in the room. I helped her back to bed. The rest of the night went without incident.

There was another time, mom believed that another resident, a lady thirty years her senior was trying to steal her legs. As I mentioned earlier, mom always had the most beautifully shaped legs. In mom's defense, the lady did threaten to use voodoo on her, according to Nikki. Of course, my sister didn't give it much credence. Several months passed. Mom made significant improvement, in terms of eating. The constant need to look after mom began to take its toll on my sister. For me, the fact that she was still on the heavy meds just didn't seem right without an underlying cause. It was time to get to the root of mom's illness. It was time to bring her back to familiar surroundings.

# "The Sandwich Generation"

## Chapter Five

It was the summer of 2007. This was also the summer that mom's siblings rallied together and drove from the mid-west to see about their sister. Mom was the oldest now. She cried when she saw Aunt Etta, Aunt Bell, Uncle Mike, Aunt Wanda, and Uncle Junior. Mom yearned for her siblings to visit for years. We were happy to see them also. With the exception of my great uncle Aubrey, a few cousins and mom's stepbrother, Jesse, we were mom's only family in the Detroit area. I spent the next several months taking mom to different doctors. I was caught in what is termed "The Sandwich Generation", which refers to a generation who is caught in the middle of raising their kids and maintaining their own lives, while also caring for their parent(s). I was caring for my mother, albeit from a distance, while still raising my then seventeen-year-old son, Dijon. My oldest son, DonLarae, was living away from home by now, working and going to school.

I started with her regular medical doctor who ordered an MRI. Tests showed some area of abnormal activity in her brain associated with memory and mood. It also revealed that mom had a mini stroke or TIA (Transient Ischemic Attack) but couldn't determine when it occurred. A TIA is a blockage of blood flow to the brain that lasts temporarily.

Unlike a full-fledged stroke, it does not cause any permanent damage but is still a serious condition.

The attack is usually over in a matter of minutes but being examined by a doctor is imperative. Wow! Finally, proof that something tangible is causing mom's problems. She's not going crazy after all! The doctor recommended that I take mom to a neurologist. So, I took her to see a neurologist at the M.I.N.D. Institute. The neurologist first wanted her to be examined by a psychologist to determine if ailment was of an organic nature or from depression. Unfortunately, mom was unable to complete certain parts of examination due to her confusion and inability to comprehend questions.

Afterwards, the neurologist ordered a dementia workup, including CAT or CT scan of the brain, EEG, and blood work. The CT scan indeed confirmed that mom had dementia. "Okay, what is it?" "And, how do we treat it?", I asked. He explained that there were different types of dementia, some reversible some not. A few can be reversed with the right diagnosis and treatment such as with a drug interaction or a vitamin deficiency. Tests also revealed that mom had plaques (clumps of protein that form on the brain) which cause the destruction of brain cells by disrupting cell-to-cell communication. This disrupts the nutrient transport to healthy brain tissues.

I was given a pamphlet that provided a broader description of Dementia and Alzheimer's Disease. I learned that Alzheimer's was the number one cause of dementia and, that there is no cure for Alzheimer's.

After receiving mom's newly confirmed diagnosis, it became clear that mom's dementia was not the irreversible type. There was no cure!

Only medication to slow the progression of the disease. Sitting on the couch in my living room one evening, I began to sob uncontrollably. Mom would never be the same.

I continued my regular routine of working throughout the week, and checking on mom periodically. Juggling an eight to ten-hour shift while managing mom's affairs had its challenges. This included, scheduling and taking mom to her doctor's appointments, the grocery store, cleaning her apartment, doing her laundry and cooking her meals. Mom just stopped cooking one day. I finally realized it was due to confusion and fear. Confusion over turning the dials on and off and fear that she would put herself in danger. Microwaveable meals became the new norm. I struggled with buying frozen dinners, which are high in sodium, versus mom being able to feed herself every day. Marie Callender's became the go-to meal as it was as close to home cooking as you could get in the frozen food section, in my humble opinion. I knew mom wouldn't eat it if it didn't taste good.

It's nearing the Fall of 2008. Mom had been able to live independently for a little over a year now. Clearly, there were signs that this would not be the reality for long. My daily calls to her would vary from day to day now. Although she was still able to answer the phone, it took longer for her to take her meds over the phone.

She struggled to take them out of the container, and at times, put in her mouth to swallow. I had to repeat instructions while encouraging her at the same time. Things began to change with each visit.

I'd notice that mom would have her shirt on backwards, or inside out. Some of the pills that I would call mom every day to take would be found on the floor where she had unknowingly dropped them. Her toothpaste would be in the kitchen cupboards instead of in the bathroom.

Mom always kept a clean house. However, that too began to change. The bathroom wasn't as clean as it used to be. The sink would be cluttered with items that were normally put neatly away, like lip stick, makeup, combs, towels, etc. The dirty clothes began to pile up. Some clean items would be mixed with unclean items. She was no longer able to sort and do her laundry. Mom would have half eaten food left in the fridge. She wasn't finishing her meals anymore. These new developments, coupled with mom's latest episode made it necessary for my brother and I to take immediate action.

Since my sister lived further away, my brother and I rushed to the hospital emergency where they had taken mom after the balcony incident. We knew that we couldn't let her go back home to her apartment but, we didn't have a suitable plan in place for her either. My home wasn't suitable for her as all three bedrooms were on the second floor. How can I keep her safe from roaming around in the middle of the night with a flight of stairs? How can I keep her at all and still work? I'm sure my brother struggled with these same thoughts.

# *"Behind Closed Doors"*

## *Chapter Six*

We didn't know what to do about mom! After checking all of her vitals, there was nothing more the doctors could do concerning her earlier episode. Mom was waiting anxiously in the emergency ward, awaiting discharge. While my brother and I were reassuring her that everything would be okay, we were frantically grappling with the hard reality…we can't let them release her…at least not tonight!

After talking to the chief physician on duty this particular night, and explaining our dilemma, we were informed that they could keep mom for a few days. They could admit her to the psych ward for an evaluation. We breathed a sigh of relief. Mom would be in a safe environment while it gave us more time to find a long-term solution. I will admit, there was some concern regarding mom's mental health. She had exhibited psychosis and hallucinations a year before while in Lansing with my sister. So, her being admitted didn't seem that farfetched.

When I went to visit her the next day, during regular visiting hours, I was denied entry into the Psych Ward. There were these two side by side steel doors that remained locked to outsiders at all times.

There was a note on door that explained its admittance policy. I was not made aware of the policy in place for new patients. No visitation was allowed for the first two days of admittance. "Oh My God!" "What Have I Done?" I need to see mom and know that she's okay.

What is her environment like? What are the sleeping arrangements? I was devastated! I felt like I let her down. How could I not know?

Two days went by. I couldn't get to the hospital fast enough! Fortunately, mom was, by all appearances, okay. Maybe a bit subdued. I sat with her in the visitor's area where some of the patients gathered. There was an older gentleman who spoke kindly of mom, saying how nice she was. Not in a flirty way, but in a sincere, genuine way. It brought a smile to mom's face. After sitting with mom for a little while, I was given a tour of the Ward. There was an area for teenagers or young adults. I remember seeing a teenager in distress, having an issue of some sort. I was led to the room where mom had slept.

One of the nurse's aides told me that mom had been crying and making references to suicide. I met with the Head of Psychiatrics to talk about a treatment plan as well as a plan for discharge. He talked about one- to-one psychotherapy, group therapy, stabilizing her and sending her back to his office for regular bi-weekly consultations. You see, we had taken mom to see him two months prior for outpatient therapy.

He adjusted her meds so that she wouldn't have hallucinations or suicidal ideations. After visiting mom on the fourth day, I was not happy to see that she was heavily medicated and in a dazed state. She was still able to move about, but had no expression, almost emotionless. I became very upset and requested that they stop giving her the new meds.

In the meantime, I began working on finding suitable housing for mom. I checked out a few Group Homes.

Recommendations I got from the Head of Psychiatrics. After visiting a few of these places, it was clearly not a place that I felt comfortable leaving mom. The oversight just wasn't the same. The homes were either gloomy looking, or didn't have anything to offer besides a bed, shower, and place to eat. These were private homes that had minimum regulatory requirements.

After obtaining a copy of the Alternatives for Seniors Magazine, I was able to identify the type of housing assistance that mom needed. The booklet categorically grouped facilities by housing type, location, amenities, and price. It had a listing for Apartments, Retirement Communities, and Nursing Homes. Then I found Assisted Living Facilities (ALF). They provide 24-hour supervision including everything from meal prep, to bathing, dressing, medication management, and recreational activities. Mom needed assistance with day-to-day activities in a safe and caring environment.

After conducting a thorough research of ALF's. We found a suitable place 20 minutes away from my brother, Punchy and his wife Sharon. We were able to take mom out of the hospital's psychiatric unit nearly three weeks after her admittance.

# *"Unwelcomed Visitor"*

## *Chapter Seven*

In November of 2008, mom's new placement was followed up with comprehensive psychiatric services every two weeks. Her new doctor was very concerned about the side effects of one of mom's medications, Abilify. He explained to me that the antipsychotic Abilify could have serious life-threatening side effects and that it wasn't recommended for dementia patients. Some of the side effects included congestive heart failure, or sudden death due to arrythmia. Other side effects included lung infections or pneumonia. As if we didn't have enough to worry about. Mom already had high blood pressure, and high cholesterol that I wasn't aware of. These alone are risk factors for strokes. So, he began to wean mom off of the medication. The doctor talked about the secondary behavioral problems associated with dementia patients, which include anxiety, agitation or combativeness. Also, symptoms including auditory or visual hallucinations, or delusions and paranoia. He started her on Namenda which was known to slow the progression of her Alzheimer's Dementia (AD). It also had a secondary calming effect that could help her behaviorally.

A few weeks had passed. Mom was already agitated from us moving her. Adrian wasn't able to visit her since he was dealing with mobility issues associated with his diabetes.

However, another male friend named Harold showed up to visit her. My brother and I had already expressed that he not see mom anymore when she was still living in her senior apartment a few months ago. I can't really remember his response, but didn't worry about him anymore after mom's placement into the facility. We just didn't trust him like we did with her friend Adrian. There was just something about Harold that seemed, suspect. One day, he called me while he and mom were out to breakfast one morning. He said, "Kim, she's not eating her food." I got on the phone with mom and asked if everything was okay. She said "yeah", but not really saying much. It wasn't long after that I received a report from a male resident who witnessed Harold pushing mom in the lobby of their senior apartment.

My reservations about him came to light. He began to drive a wedge between us and mom. She started accusing us of stealing her money and other items. We instructed the facility administrators and aides to not allow him visitation because it was inciting mom to act out. Harold was trying to talk mom into marrying him. Clearly, something was wrong with him to even think she was capable of taking care of herself, let alone, be married. Obviously, it was for his own selfish reasons. There was no way in hell this was going to happen! He ignored our requests to stop seeing her. He kept showing up at the facility as if he was her man! The facility administrators said that legally, they could not keep him from visiting her. We would have to get a restraining order to keep him out.

We petitioned Probate Court for a Hearing to stop him from coming anywhere near her. He even had the audacity to show up at the Courthouse! I saw him in the parking lot as I was walking towards the building. The judge ruled on our behalf! For some odd reason, Harold never made it to the Courtroom. I have to believe it was *Divine Intervention* because he finally stayed away from mom. I'm sure it bothered him to see her there. It bothered us too! He probably believed he would be helping her by getting married. Mom confided in me one day when she had clarity. She believed Harold wanted to marry her so they could combine their monthly retirement income. Mom said her income was way more than his. Didn't She call it!

# *"Settling Down"*

## *Chapter Eight*

Up to this point, I had Medical Durable Power-of-Attorney for mom. I had authority to speak on behalf of her medical affairs. I had already been handling her personal affairs, I just needed to have it in writing. In early June of 2009, I picked mom up from the facility and took her out to lunch. This is something we did regularly throughout her residency. During the end of our meal, I mentioned to mom that I went to Court that morning and was granted legal guardianship. Mom became agitated and started to say how tired she was of the whole thing (i.e. people telling her what to do, when to go, etc.). She also started making references to suicide. My heart sunk. What I thought would be received with some acceptance, wasn't! Then again, maybe a part of me knew she wouldn't react favorably which is why I waited to the end of our meal to tell her. I just wanted mom to know what was going on concerning her welfare. Clearly, there was still a part of her that was fighting for every ounce of independence and power she had left.

Eventually things calmed down. Her mood swings began to stabilize and mellow out with the adjustments to her meds. Mom settled into her environment. She shared a room with another resident. It became harder to leave mom with each visit.

I wanted so desperately to take her out of there for good. Bringing her home during holidays and special occasions was always bittersweet because it would be time to take her back. She has been through so much! It just didn't seem fair!

Well, one thing I could appreciate about the facility was its beautifully landscaped grounds. The one-story brick building was surrounded by a lot of green space. There was a walkway that circled the building. Mom and I walked that path many times during her four-year stay. We had plenty of talks outdoors near the pond where geese gathered. For the most part, the facility was well managed.

Despite the high turnover of aides, the staff were very attentive to mom. Most of the residents in the Memory Care Ward were much older than mom. Those who were able to walk around freely went in and out of each other's rooms. Many times, they would forget whose room they were in and move items around. A few of mom's shoes would disappear periodically. The laundry was the worst. Mom's clothes would come back color washed or shrunk. Some of her items would be missing like a shirt, socks, and pants. Sometimes someone else's items would be found in mom's laundry.

Although her items were labeled, it wasn't error proof. I complained about it often. Sadly because of the distance and my work schedule, it was just too much for me to take her laundry home and get it back in a timely manner. After nearly two years, mom was no longer able to hold the phone long enough to have a conversation.

When we called, the aides would seat her near the phone. Mom would hold the phone for a few seconds. She would answer, then soon after we began a conversation, mom's concentration and focus began to wane. She would take the phone from her ear and hold it or drop it in her lap. So, our communication concerning her was limited to talking to the aides and asking them how mom was doing.

Hospice got involved in mom's care on and off as changes in Medicaid coverage fluctuated from one year to another. They had volunteers do mom's nails, read to her, and sometimes just sit with her for companionship. These services really helped as they provided another set of eyes when we couldn't be there.

# "Get Set! Ready! Go!"

## Chapter Nine

It's been nearly four years now since mom has been in the Assisted Living Facility (ALF). The calls regarding her falls had become more frequent, and more alarming! They would report her falling and then being unresponsive. EMS would be called and would rush her to the emergency room. I would get the call while at work and rushed to the hospital thinking the worse! Once there, I would find mom conscious and sitting up in bed stable and alert. This happened on two occasions! One too many, for my heart. Of course, I'm happy and relieved, but my emotions were like a rollercoaster concerning mom. Up and down! I knew it was time to move mom. Her frequent falls was a sign that her care was becoming too much for the ALF staff.

I started preparing, mentally, to leave the City two years prior but knew that I needed to hang in there a little while longer. I remember reading Rick Warren's "Purpose Driven Life", fifteen years earlier. It's a book about our life's purpose. There was a passage in the book that talked about people and retirement. He said that people shouldn't look forward to working thirty or more years as a reward for their life's work, but instead seek God and His purpose for our life which is the greatest reward bestowed upon man! From then on, I told myself I would work just long enough to earn a pension.

At 25 years, I had planned to retire and seek my passion. Oh, I enjoyed my career as an Assessing Officer of Real Property. I just wasn't passionate about it. After 26 years, I was ready to go! I was ready to step out on faith in pursuit of something more fulfilling. Something more purposeful. I knew I needed to get ready for something. Not sure of what exactly, only that I needed to get ready!

In October of 2012, I put in my two-week notice. It was time! I packed my belongings and bid my farewells. I left on the 29th and went in for a hysterectomy on the 30th. I planned it all accordingly. I got tired of looking like I was four months pregnant every month during my menstrual cycle. The fibroid tumors I've had for nearly thirty years began to wear on me. For years they never really bothered me. So, the doctors didn't bother them. In the last year and a half, I began to feel pressure in my lower abdomen. I made plans! I had things to do! I need to be in the best shape possible.

The procedure went well. I was at home recovering, settling into my new normal. Two weeks into my recovery, I received a phone call concerning mom. The head administrator of the ALF informed me that mom had been having too many falls recently. She said they didn't feel they could adequately keep her safe. Therefore, I was given a two week notice of her discharge from the facility. Shocked at the timing, but not surprised. I knew I needed to get ready for her, I just wasn't expecting it to be so soon. I thought I had more time.

A few months maybe. When mom had her last fall, I questioned the circumstances surrounding it. If she is being monitored, why is she falling? I was told that an aide was standing right next to her when she fell the last time. They would say that she would be walking around for long periods, or standing looking out the window. I questioned why was she allowed to walk around for long periods. I questioned the length of time she would be left standing. That's why she was there, for 24-hour supervision! After further dialogue, the administrator expressed her concern for my situation. She then explained that mom's falls were causing emotional stress to the aides because she would become unresponsive. I didn't argue. I thanked her for the care they had provided for the past four years. I then asked for an extra two weeks before they discharged mom so that I could have more time to make arrangements.

After mom's last fall, I was concerned for her safety. Not so much, that she wasn't being watched, but more that her Alzheimer's was progressing to the point that it was a danger for her to even walk or stand without assistance. I spoke with a geriatric specialist while in the hospital after mom's last fall. I asked about her falling and if it was common with her ailment. The doctor said that it was, in fact, common with dementia patients and, that it may worsen with time.

# *"Homeward Bound"*

## *Chapter Ten*

What do I do now! I couldn't bear the thought of putting mom somewhere else. I didn't have the energy to search for a suitable facility. She is my mother! Afterall! With considerable thought, I began to rationalize. My current home is roomier! I could convert my study into an area for mom! I didn't have to worry about her going up and down the stairs, like with the old house! Mom needs to be loved on! She deserves to be with her family! It's time to bring her home!

I talked with my husband about the idea of bringing mom home. He was very supportive for the most part, but also knew that it would be a huge undertaking. I didn't know how I would be able to manage, but trusted that God would make a way. I started making a list of things needed to make mom's space her own. A bed, dresser, and her favorite curtains that she used to have hanging in the bathroom over the tub in her house. It was a beautiful cream-colored sheer curtain with embroidered red roses and green stems. Mom also had a matching quilt that I put on the full-sized bed. The walls were already painted a sage shade of green with an accent wall the color of a dark green olive. I was so excited! I knew mom would love her new room, her new home!

There were other things I needed to take care of. I talked with Sue, a Hospice Care Manager who had been involved in mom's care at the ALF.

She put me in touch with MORC (Macomb-Oakland Regional Center) Home Care, Inc., which is a State and Federally funded non-profit organization in Michigan. They have Support Coordinators who come out to your home to do an assessment for in-home services. They help you put together a "Plan of Care". They assessed my home to make sure it was safe for mom to move around.

They also approved me for the MI Choice Medicaid Waiver Program so that I could enroll mom in an adult daycare a few times a week to give me a break. Everything was falling into place. I went to Benson's, a medical supply store to purchase a toilet seat with handles for mom. MORC connected me to a supplier that delivered wipes, gloves, and briefs monthly and, the Support Coordinators facilitated transfer of mom's prescriptions to my home address. It was a lot that needed to be done, but I was willing to give it a try. I felt, it was the least I could do.

The day has arrived! She's home! I brought mom home! After I got her things situated, mom began to walk around the main part of the house that included the living room, kitchen, and her newly decorated bedroom in the study. She began to look around, walking with her arms slightly folded. By the second day, her posture even improved. She was standing straighter and not slightly bent over like before.

Mom started smiling more every time she saw me. She even began to try to talk more, even though her sentences were somewhat fragmented. I let her walk around for a while so she could get familiar with her new surroundings.

I was over-joyed at the thought of not having to see her in that place. I realized at that very moment, me moving her was as much for my sanity as it was for hers. I needed to see if she would thrive! If the Alzheimer's had progressed to the last stage, I wanted to be the last stop! I feared her being alone, without any family by her side when the good Lord calls her home. I Am My Mother's Keeper!!!

As the evenings set in, I tucked mom into bed with a kiss goodnight. Mom smiled each time. Now, I knew she felt loved! I settled into my daily routine with her. I woke up in the middle of the night to walk her to the bathroom. That way, her briefs wouldn't be entirely soaked by the time I got her up in the morning. The same with administering her medications, and feeding mom. I made her oatmeal, coffee, bacon, toast, etc. I made sure to keep fruit on hand, like bananas, apples, strawberries. Dinner was also a joy! Mom still had a healthy appetite. I loved making her favorite pinto beans and cornbread, or rice and vegetables, and chicken. Mom loved sucking on a chicken bone! She always did.

The days came and went. I started feeling fatigued by late afternoons. I was still recovering from my hysterectomy a month earlier and adjusting to my new routine. I would recline mom on the couch, turn on the radio to some gospel, then recline myself in the loveseat and take a nap.

I knew she wouldn't be able to get up on her own with the way the couch was designed. So, it was safe to take a nap nearby. I would awake an hour or so later and find mom sitting back watching me.

Once, I woke to say, "I'm sorry momma, I needed a nap". She responded, "That's okay". Other days, she napped with me on and off.

# "Sarah Really does Care"

## Chapter Eleven

Two weeks later, I took mom to Sarah Care. An adult daycare about 20 minutes away. I felt a good vibe about the environment and the services they provided. For instance, the place was clean, colorful and well organized. They had adequate staffing, and showers on hand to bathe the adults if needed. A chef was on hand to prepare the meals daily for breakfast and lunch. Everyone had their own separate locker for their personal belongings. They offered crafts, pet therapy, music therapy, and dance therapy.

The staff were very professional and interacted with mom in a caring manner. It was a dream come true! Just as much as I needed the reprieve, mom needed the socialization. I got her registered to attend three days a week for up to nine hours a day. There was also a nurse or two on duty to administer certain medications and do weekly blood pressure checks. I scheduled mom to attend on Mondays, Wednesdays, and Fridays. She loved it! On some rides to and from, I would have the radio on in the car. Mom would get to rocking and moving to the beat of the music. Sometimes we stopped at the store on the way home to pick up some items, like her Ensure protein shakes, and whatever else was needed.

Mom was able to hold on and push the cart. My husband, Don and I seemed to have been adjusting fairly well.

It also helped that the Michigan Department of Health & Human Services approved us for mom's monthly Social Security Income to help cover monthly expenses, like rent, gas, electric, food and clothing. I set aside approximately 20% to put into a savings account for mom. Of course, all of these expenditures had to be accounted for at the end of the year, so I made sure to use it wisely.

Don and I bowl on a league twice a month on Sunday afternoons. We've been a part of the league for several years. It was very important that we maintained our regularly scheduled time together. I contacted a Homecare Agency in the area to provide assistance on our bowling Sundays. They sent someone the following week for us to get to know them for a few days before we left them alone with mom. They were usually young adult females. I signed off on a checklist of all the things I needed help with, like feeding mom dinner, folding and putting away her laundry, or putting her to bed. On the first two scheduled appointments, she came through. By the third appointment, the agency notified me that they had to send a new homecare worker because the other girl quit. The second homecare worker stayed for about a month.

By the time we got to a third caregiver, I no longer trusted the agency. We became concerned about having all these different people in our home—alone! We weren't willing to risk having someone in our home we couldn't trust. I received a recommendation of another homecare agency and they sent us an older lady who was reliable and stayed for the duration of our bowling season. After three months of mom being home, she had a fall in the living room.

I was in the kitchen prepping food when I heard a loud thump! I walked in the direction of the sound and found mom lying on the floor, on her side near the front door. She didn't make a sound.

No scream. No tears. She just laid there. I picked her up and starting talking to her to ask her how she felt. I walked her slowly to the couch and watched her facial expressions. She was slightly wincing. I knew then that I needed to take her to the emergency room. It turned out mom had a hip fracture. They admitted her and scheduled her for surgery the next day. Fortunately, she didn't require hip replacement, just a few screws to put in place to help her mend. How did this happen? How did mom fall on a flat surface? Did she stumble? Trip?

I kept imagining the scene over in my head. I was careful to not have her on her feet for long periods of time. There are four steps that leads to a landing to the right of the entry way. I concluded that mom must have stepped on one or two of the steps and lost her balance and fell over on her side. I felt awful! I was supposed to keep her safe. I should have put up a barrier. When

I observed mom walking in that area on many occasions, she would always stop and turn in the other direction. I realized then that I had been so focused on creating a normal experience for mom, when in fact, she wasn't normal. She couldn't perceive danger.

The crazy thing about mom's dementia is that she never displayed any emotion besides the wincing. Even then, it was very minimal. The surgery went well. No additional problems.

After a few days in recovery, mom was transferred to a rehab facility at another location and remained there for approximately six weeks. We visited her several times a week and were able to watch her progress during rehab. Mom's strength improved with each therapy session. On some days after the end of his work day, Don would stop by to check on mom and help feed her dinner.

# *"A Rush to Judgement"*

## *Chapter Twelve*

Mom was back home. Fortunately, she was still able to bare weight. I couldn't allow mom to walk freely around the house. She would have to have someone walk with her. So, when I or my husband, Don couldn't walk with her, we would have her sitting down. By about the ninth month, mom began to lose the ability to feed herself. I began to spoon feed her. Her appetite was still strong, however. The six weeks mom spent in rehab created pressure ulcers on her heels. It took weeks to heal. It required constant repositioning of her feet, especially when she slept at night. Every time I elevated or repositioned mom's feet, she would move them right back to her comfort zone.

It became increasingly difficult to get mom in and out of bed. I had to replace her regular bed with a hospital bed that adjusted up and down to help with easing her in and out. Then, mom started losing the ability to bend her knees when walking up and down the stairs. Even getting her in and out of the car became difficult. Don and I ended up having a wheelchair ramp built off the garage. It became necessary to wheel her in and out of the house.

Aunt Etta, came to visit her for about a week or so. Mom seemed to recognize her voice. Aunt Etta would call mom's name, "Laura!" Mom would answer loudly, "What!" Uncle Mike and his wife, Aunt Lori also came to see mom. She exhibited some moments of clarity.

They were concerned about my well-being by now. I guess I couldn't hide the fact that it worried me their sister wasn't getting any better. I knew I couldn't give her the quality care she so desperately required. I was dealing with the pain and frustration of having to let her go and, the last thing I wanted was to put her back in a nursing facility.

Mom declined to the point that a trip to the emergency room became almost routine. On the last trip to emergency, I cried while sitting next to her as she was being treated for a UTI (Urinary Tract Infection). A UTI can throw a dementia patient's system completely off-kilter. I knew then that it was time to let her go. We have had so many people in and out of our home—from homecare physicians, to equipment couriers, to Emergency Medical Technician's (EMT's), to homecare coordinators, to homecare aides—that the idea of providing long-term care for mom was insurmountable. I continued to meet with the homecare coordinators from MORC. I expressed the need for them to assist me with finding a suitable placement for mom, only not in a nursing facility, but a licensed group home.

I thought mom would adjust better by being in a home-like setting, since she had been with me for a year. They left it up to me to find a home then they would facilitate the placement, if it met the criteria. I was given the name of 'A Place for Mom' from a listing of resources I received months earlier. I called to set up appointments to view several group home facilities no more than a half hour's drive from me.

I had time to look while mom was recovering at another rehab facility to regain her strength after being in the hospital for a week, recovering from the UTI infection.

After looking at several group homes, I found what seemed to be a suitable home setting for mom. The home was nice and clean, and beautiful and spacious. The owner, Eleanor had a couple of group homes she managed. MORC conducted a home inspection after the owner submitted all the documentation and paperwork requested. A few days after Christmas of 2013, we moved mom from rehab to the group home. About a week later, we were able to celebrate mom's 70th birthday in her new placement on January 7th, with cake and balloons. It was a good day.

A couple of weeks later, with observation, I noticed the aide doing too much when caring for mom, especially when she had to move her and bathe her. There were six residents to one aide. I started asking questions concerning her having help to care for mom. She would always say, "I don't need help." Before mom's placement, I was told by the owner that she would have two people to care for the residents, including mom.

I also began to inquire about mom's diet after I saw that she was being given pop to sip on with a straw on several occasions.

Mom should have been sipping on something more nutritional like a protein shake or juice which was on her list of diets I provided to the owner.

On mom's first day of placement, Eleanor cooked a nice dinner and had me believe that she did most of the cooking. It turned out that the homecare aide did the cooking, the medication management, and care of the residents. I started inquiring about mom's care with the owner and aide. Especially since mom's monthly allowance covered the cost of two aides and, after I would find mom lying awake in bed the majority of the time, in a room by herself, while other residents would be up sitting in the living room watching TV with the homecare aide sitting right next to them.

# *"Blessed Assurance"*

## *Chapter Thirteen*

It was March 5, 2014 when I got ready for bed. In search for some 'food for thought' and prayer, I opened my bible to the 23rd Psalm. I stored a swatch of mom's hair that came out when I combed it several weeks ago at the group home. I remember being so upset that I balled it up and put it in my pocket. I could still smell the sweet fragrance of her hair cream. I placed it there in preparation for mom's transition. Four weeks prior, a dream revealed the Lord told momma she had seven weeks. Seven weeks for what? I thought as I awoke from the dream. I went to check the calendar for seven weeks from the date.

The thought of having to move my mother again terrified me as she seems to decline more with each move. The thought of having to police another facility, just to ensure some quality of care, zapped me of all my energy. It turned out the aide complained to the owner about my questioning her care of mom. I requested a meeting. The aide demanded that either I go, or she goes! I had until the end of the month to remove mom from the group home. It was exactly seven weeks to the date of my dream. Lord, Jesus!

By now, I realized, it was time to stop! Stop trying to handle things in my own power. I was tired. Disappointed. Defeated. I got my brother and sister on board and enlisted their support in finding a suitable long-term placement for mom.

After checking out several nursing home facilities, someone recommended Lahser Hills Care Center to Punchy. After checking it out, we moved mom in. She remained there for two years. We continued to love her with each visit, each birthday, and each holiday. I still monitored her care. Fortunately, it didn't require a lot of policing. The facility was well-managed, well equipped to care for her, and the staff was very professional. Mom's health, weight, and appearance improved after placement.

She enjoyed music therapy, watching TV, and me taking her outside for some fresh air. We all had our own routines. Punchy, an ordained minister, faithfully prayed over her. Nikki enjoyed reading to her. I enjoyed stimulating her with touch, like rubbing her hands, arms, face, and hair. On March 6, 2016, I got the call that mom had stopped eating. Two days later, mom was called home to Glory! I was right there with her. I had prayed for God to give me a sign when that day would come. But, God's word says, *"...of that day and hour knoweth no man, no, not the angels of heaven, but my Father only" (Mathew 24:36 KJV).* I never wanted her to be alone. A month before, I had a dream. God gave me a vision of seeing mom take her last breath. I knew it was his way of preparing me and assuring me that I didn't need to worry about her being alone. That vision played out. I was right there, by her side. Mom wasn't alone. To God Be the Glory!

# 3-Common Types of Dementia

**Dementia** - **is not** a specific disease, but rather a broad term for neurological conditions that involve some form of serious mental impairment, such as memory loss, confusion, and/or personality changes. About 20% of dementia can be reversed, with the rest being irreversible and tending to worsen with time. *(www.diffen.com)*

**Alzheimer's Disease (AD)** is the most common irreversible cause of dementia. It is a degenerative brain disease that destroys memory and other important mental functions. The disease produces physical changes in the brain, with some areas shrinking and others widening. When parts of the brain shrink or widen, the normal connections inside are broken, disrupting electrical signals in the brain. It accounts for 50% to 70% of all dementia cases. *(www.diffen.com)*

**Vascular Dementia** is the second most common cause of dementia which accounts for 17% of cases. According to the Alzheimer's Association, it occurs from blood vessel blockage or damage leading to strokes or bleeding in the brain. The onset may occur suddenly. Symptoms include impaired judgement, difficulties concentrating, and problems with planning and organization. *(www.GoodTherapy.org)*

**Pseudodementia** is a type of cognitive impairment that mimics dementia but actually occurs due to the presence of a mood-related mental health concern, which is most often depression. This condition is usually seen in older individuals. *(www.GoodTherapy.org)*

**Causes of a Transient Ischemic Attack (TIA)** is high blood pressure. Other reasons one may experience a TIA is a blood clot which narrows the blood vessels in and around the brain. Other causes are diabetes, and high cholesterol. Symptoms are the same, or very similar to those of a life-threatening stroke (i.e. numbness and paralysis of the face, arm, or down an entire side of the body). Also slurred speech, and blurred vision. Some may experience complete blindness, double vision, a severe headache out of nowhere and a loss of balance.

A Rutgers University study estimates that approximately 4% of Americans between 65 and 74 years old have Alzheimer's disease, with the percentage steadily rising as we age. The same research estimates that approximately 50% of all Americans over the age of 85 suffer with Alzheimer's disease and more than half of all dementia cases are misdiagnosed and are actually Alzheimer's Disease. *(www.facty.com)*

# 15 Early Warning Signs of Dementia

1. **Agitation** – Occurs gradually, leads to anger, embarrassment, social withdrawal.

2. **Apathy and Withdrawal** – Losing interest in things they previously enjoyed like hobbies or favorite activities.

3. **Behavioral Changes** – Early stages of Alzheimer's. Becoming anxious, depressed, irritable due to confusion and fear.

4. **Cognitive Decline** – Can enter in the mid and later stages of the disease, resulting in trouble with memory. Performance of mundane daily tasks, losing objects, the inability to use the right word, forgetting names or people, dates, and organizational skills.

5. **Declining Motor Function** – Lose the physical ability to perform routine tasks (i.e. operate the stove, drive to grocery store, and need 24-hour care for their safety.

6. **Difficulty w/Complex Tasks and Abstract Thinking** – Having trouble balancing a checkbook or understanding the numbers on a calculator.

7. **Disorganization** – Can't find eyeglasses.

8. **Disorientation** – Getting lost on routine trip.

9. **Disrupted Sleep** – Not sleeping through the night.

10. **Hallucinations** – Or delusional thoughts. Most commonly visual (seeing things that are not there). Patients with Alzheimer's can actually feel, hear, see, taste, and smell things that don't really exist.

11. **Impaired Judgement** – Choice of clothing, driving poorly.

12. **Memory Loss** – Or Mild Cognitive Impairment (MCI) which is more pronounced than the typical age-related forgetfulness.

13. **Paranoia** – Becoming delusional and suspicious of those around them.

14. **Reduced Concentration** – Trouble focusing. Can also be difficult to follow storylines on movies and TV shows.

15. **Sexual Actions** – It's common for dementia patients to suddenly become sexual without being aware that their actions are inappropriate. For example, removing clothing, exposing oneself in public, or touching or saying tasteless things to strangers and caregivers. This happens when damage becomes more severe in the brain's frontal and temporal lobes, which is the area that manages control responses.

*(Warning Signs derived from Emily Lockhart of www.Activebeat.com)*

# *Afterword*

*I experienced all of the above-noted warning signs with my mother, Laura, spanning over ten years. Looking back, there are some things mom exhibited several years before signs and symptoms became more evident.*

*It should be noted that the only way to confirm Alzheimer's Disease is by performing an autopsy of the brain. For this reason, many doctors will use the dementia label when diagnosing patients. It wasn't until Laura's continuous decline and the need for healthcare providers to give a specific diagnosis of her decline that doctors called it Alzheimer's. It is not clear if doctors were able to pinpoint the exact cause of her dementia (i.e. stress, depression, stroke).*

*I initially believed the layoff from her job set the ball in motion that led to the loss of her home, which sent her into a deep depression. However, I learned later that mom was actually laid-off because she was forgetting things like machine parts, moving too slow, and exchanging words with her supervisor. She had already started exhibiting signs of confusion and agitation. Tests clearly show that she suffered a mini stroke or TIA's that went undetected, causing more damage. Her long history of hypertension combined with her high cholesterol may have triggered the domino effect.*

I pray this book will not only serve as a guide for you to recognize the signs and symptoms of Alzheimer's/dementia, but will empower you to become an advocate for the fight against Alzheimer's Disease.

**For more information on Alzheimer's & Dementia call the 24/7 Helpline at: (800-272-3900), or go to:**

**www.alz.org**

**www.diffen.com/difference/Alzheimer**

**www.mayoclinic.org/diseases-conditions/alzheimers-disease**

# *About Author*

    Kimberly J. Richardson is a retired City of Detroit assessor of real property. After embarking on a journey in search of her passion, Kimberly encountered ageism in the workplace. It wasn't long after that she would lose her long-anticipated healthcare and other benefits in a bankruptcy declared by the City that Kimberly's purpose found her. She became concerned about her quality of life, and set out to help others enjoy the same. She is the founder of 50plusshadesofus.com, a platform created for people 50 and older to *Show How Age Doesn't End Seasons*. From there was birthed *Shades of Glory* where Kimberly coach purpose-driven individuals 50 and older to tell their story by sharing their *Seasons of Promise, Perseverance, and Praise*.

My Mother's Keeper is a story that chronicles her journey with her mother's nearly ten-year battle with Alzheimer's Disease.

Kimberly pledges to donate a percentage of proceeds from the sale of her books to the Alzheimer's Association to aide in their research for a cure to end the devastating disease.

She can be reached at www.50plusshadesofus.com or by email at info@50plusshadesofus.com.

**Book Kimberly J. Richardson: She's available to speak at your first or next event!!**

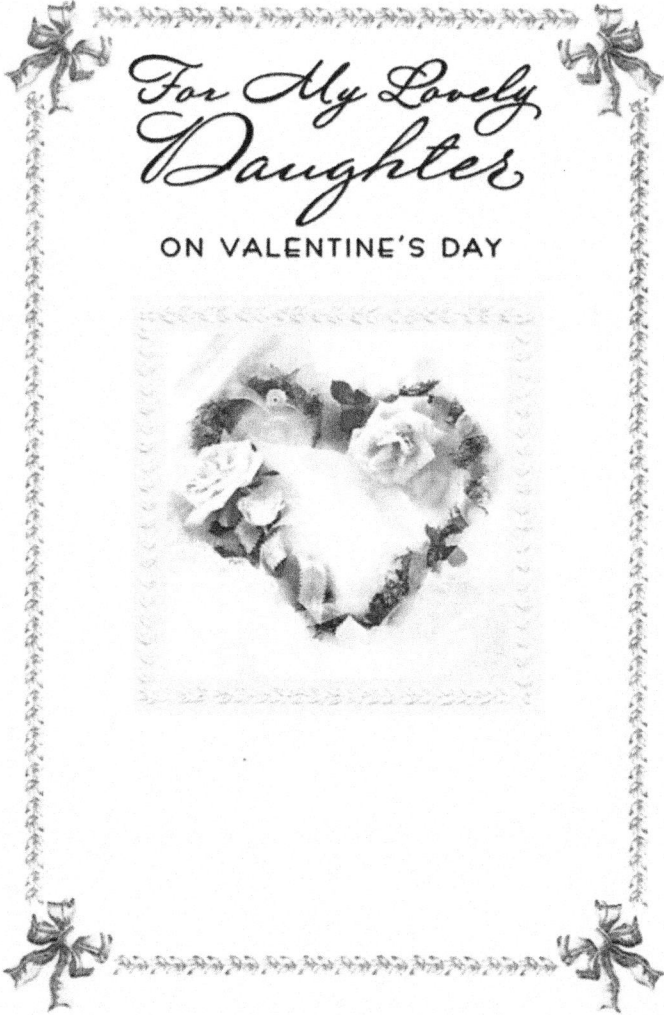

For My Lovely Daughter

ON VALENTINE'S DAY

Kim,

No one can count on the future
or know what they someday might do.
But could I have chosen a daughter,
my heart would have reached out for you--
I'd have wished for your warm disposition
and dreamed of your spirit and style,
I'd have hoped for your love and affection,
imagined your beautiful smile...

Life holds some gifts
and surprises,
and one of the best
there could be
is having a daughter as lovely
as the one who was given to me.

Happy
Valentine's Day

Love,
Mom

*For a Special Daughter*

Dear Kim,

You're a dear daughter
and a wonderful person.
Maybe that sounds
like parents talking —
but then, who else could
know you better?

Who else could be so aware
of all the things
about you that make you
so special and so unique?
You're a daughter to be
really proud of,
and you're loved more
than you know.

Happy Birthday
Love,
Mom